SURGE

# SURGE

Jay Bernard

Chatto & Windus
LONDON

5 7 9 10 8 6 4

Chatto & Windus, an imprint of Vintage,
20 Vauxhall Bridge Road,
London SW1V 2SA

Chatto & Windus is part of the Penguin Random House group of companies
whose addresses can be found at global.penguinrandomhouse.com.

First published in the UK by Chatto & Windus in 2019

penguin.co.uk/vintage

A CIP catalogue record for this book is available from the British Library

ISBN 9781784742614

Typeset in 11/14 pt Minion
by Integra Software Services Pvt. Ltd, Pondicherry

Printed and bound in Great Britain by Clays Ltd, Elcograf S.p.A.

Penguin Random House is committed to a sustainable future for our business,
our readers and our planet. This book is made from Forest Stewardship
Council® certified paper.

"You've seen the physical. I was dealing with the opposite medium. I was in the belly of the beast ... when you have to collect information and walk back into the belly of the beast to put it over, you're on dangerous grounds."
– ALEX PASCALL, NEW CROSS FIRE REMEMBRANCE, ALBANY, DEPTFORD, 2011

"For here we have not an enduring city, but we are looking for the city to come." – HEBREWS 13:14

# Contents

*Author's Note* ix
Arrival 1
Ark 2
Patois 4
Harbour 5
Songbook 7
Clearing 11
+ 13
– 14
Kitchen 15
Proof 17
Window 19
Duppy 22
Hiss 25
Washing 26
Stone 28
Apple 29
Songbook II 30
Pem-People 34
Pace 36
Tympanum 37
Ha-my-ca 38
Kombucha 41
Peg 42
Pride 43
Sentence 45
Ark II 46
Chemical 47
Blank 48
Baccy 50
Losers 51
Flowers 53

*Notes* 55
*Acknowledgements* 57

# Author's Note

In 2016, I was invited to be writer in residence at the George Padmore Institute, an archive, library and research centre dedicated to radical black history in Britain. At the back of my mind, I knew that I was interested in the New Cross Fire. It was only when I opened the boxes relating to it that I realised I had grown up as a black British Londoner with a piecemeal understanding of the event and the consequences that followed.

In the early hours of Sunday morning, on 18 January 1981, a fire broke out at 439 New Cross Road. It was Yvonne Ruddock's sixteenth birthday, and she had arranged a party with her cousin to celebrate. The fire spread quickly, killing thirteen young people and injuring twenty-seven others.

In the immediate aftermath of the fire, dubbed the 'New Cross Massacre', many believed it had been a racist attack. Investigations yielded little: early reports by the police indicated that an incendiary device was found under the window. Forensics experts later said the fire had started in the middle of the room. Some of the teenagers who had been at the party gave statements that they later retracted in court, saying they had been intimidated or coerced. In response to the police investigation, a group of activists called the New Cross Massacre Action Committee conducted their own interviews – and these are largely the ones that inform this book.

There was near silence from the government and the press. This had been the climate for many years: families being burned out of their homes, migrants attacked and murdered in the street. The police were at best indifferent and at worst party to the hostility.

On 2 March 1981, thousands of black people and their allies gathered at Fordham Park in Lewisham. It came to be known as the Black People's Day of Action and was the largest political gathering of black people in British history at the time. Organised by underacknowledged British activists such as John La Rose, Darcus Howe, Sybil Phoenix, Alex Pascall and many others, the intended route went from Lewisham to Hyde Park. It was raining. No demonstration had crossed a bridge in London for centuries. As the demonstration approached Blackfriars, the police tried to push the crowds back. People ran. This flowed into Fleet Street, once home of the media, where journalists leaned out of the windows and spat and jeered at the march.

After a belated response to the deaths of the thirteen young people (addressed to the activists, not the families), a police initiative began in retaliation to the Black People's Day of Action, and ostensibly to curb crime in South London. The hated SUS laws gave licence to SWAMP 81, an operation in which close to a thousand black and ethnic minority people were stopped and searched in South London in five days. The name of the operation was seen as an insensitive reference to Thatcher's 1978 speech in which she said, "People are really rather afraid, that this country might be rather swamped by people with a different culture … people are going to react and be rather hostile to those coming in."

During the tense time of SWAMP 81, the attempted arrest of a man who had been stabbed prompted the Brixton uprising in April 1981, also known as the Brixton riots. Since the blame for this lay firmly at the door of the police, an investigation was commissioned producing the Scarman Report, 'The Brixton Disorders 10–12 April 1981'; it found the police guilty of causing the riots due to its refusal to listen to the community it was supposed to serve. This triggered a new era in race relations in the UK, in conjunction with the ongoing activism and resistance of the black, Asian and ethnic minority organising groups.

My residency began just after the Brexit vote. As I read through the interviews, looked at the photos, listened to the audio, watched the footage, it struck me that the events of the present were eerily similar to the events up to and after the New Cross Fire. Then in June 2017, Grenfell happened. Institutional indifference to working class lives had left nearly eighty people dead. The Windrush scandal was reminiscent of right-wing calls for black repatriation. The archive became, for me, a mirror of the present, a much-needed instruction manual to navigate what felt like the repetition of history. The most chilling aspect of this was the lack of closure, the lack of responsibility and the lack of accountability at the centre of both the New Cross Fire and Grenfell. And the more I read and discussed, the more vexed the relationship between public narration and private truths appeared. I realised I was one of many who had visited the archives and come to a similar conclusion about the tragic and ill-concluded nature of the case. Many questions emerged not only about memory and history, but about my place in Britain as a queer black person. This opened out into a final sense of coherence: I am from here, I am specific to this place, I am haunted by this history but I also haunt it back.

SURGE

# Arrival

remember we were brought here from the clear waters of our dreams

that we might be named, numbered and forgotten

that we were made visible that we might be looked on with contempt

that they gave us their first and last names that we might be called wogs

and to their minds made flesh that it might be stripped from our backs

kept hungry that we might cry in our children's sleep

close our smoky mouths around their dreams

swallow them as they gaze upon us

never to be full –


snap, crackle

amen

# Ark

Now shall we consult the life of a stranger?
Now shall we see what can and cannot be kept?

I take this morning from its box, see how the years have warped
its edges, its middle pages conjoined at the text.

I remove the rusted paper clip, dry-sponge its brittle red remains,
unfold a liver-spotted note in copper ink,

date it by the flaking Letraset and amber glue,
press each part to the flatbed scanner,

wonder which words to file
the damp smoke and young bones under.


\*


I sometimes recognise a face from a Hi8 film,

am introduced to she-who-squatted-in-the-seventies,
who-made-that-speech, who remembers '81

when a crowd black as my hand gathered one morning,
came over Blackfriars Bridge, were heckled by the press.

The year was still fresh,
still screaming with its eyes closed,

*Mi brudda dead, mi brudda dead, mi brudda dead-o*
*Mi sista dead, mi sista dead, mi sista dead-o*

A white-sleeved hack hung from that ledge to better spit at
some kid who recalls it by their cup of archive wine.

\*

I take this January morning in my hands and wonder
if it should go under London, England, Britain, British, Black-British –

where to put the burning house, the child made ash, the brick in the back
of the neck, the shit in the letter box and piss up the side of it?

I file it under *fire, corpus, body, house.*

# Patois

I heard a sound on New Cross Road that took me back:
the first clause of a cuss sprayed from a custom Golf M2,
three Asian boys near the Five Bells pub spoke

as if we had grown up side-by-side,
sudden cousins,
taking turns to lick each other with
*bloodclart!* when someone took your ludi piece,
*raatid!* like there was no money this month,
*awoh!* when someone suffered in a way we could enjoy.

Like the *t* in *wa'er*, the absent *farver*, like *pouring bear*,
South London kids
would part suspend
their mother tongue
sobbing after someone cussed their mum,
and come to sound exactly

like my mother
screaming *yu rass* at a shocked white face –

They don't understand what I'm saying, she said.
Which is why she said it, knowing they felt every word.
They watched us, pursed and spat as we do.

Now ginger kids *yam dumplins*, hijabis snub *the man dem* –

This century dubbed by migrants from the last.
We do not speak with one voice about one thing
below the yellow, black and green flag of England.

# Harbour

my voice

                it was so weak, so sickened,
      so grieved,

my voice it was so weak
and it broke in the heat, so sickened,

so sad, my voice it was broke, so low
was the hope, that it sickened,

I choked,

it closed in my throat,

    my voice it was weak,

so sickened, so grieved –

                my voice became glass
        breaking in heat

I called
        and no-one seemed to call with me

no-one seemed to know or see
          what I had seen –

        I was so sickened and so grieved

and I said to the child I knew
harboured in the fire – jump

        Yvonne, jump Paul, jump –

        and I said to my god I knew
            harboured in the fire – jump

        Yvonne, jump Paul, jump –

                I said, I called – jump

Yvonne, jump Paul, jump –

my voice it was so weak

                – Paul, jump –

                so sickened and so grieved.

# Songbook

Me seh ah one step fahwahd an ah two step back
Me seh ah tree step fahwahd an ah six step back
Me seh ah four step fahwahd an ah one step back
Me seh ah one half fahwahd an ah one half back

Me seh ah left side fahwahd an me right side back
Bust up left side right side haffi change tack
Me seh half de revalushun deh pun de attack
Only half a salushun to de tings dem we lack

Me seh gyal love reggae an gyal love move
Bwoy love reggae an im love up im groove
Di two ah dem rub up an starting to move
Crowd gone quiet, people stop nyam dem food

An dem watch and dem see this wicked emcee
This beautiful gyal all dress up in green
Nails done nice, hair cris, wha yuh mean
Di baddest likkle gyal dem evah did see

Me seh ah one step fahwahd an ah two step back
Me seh ah tree step fahwahd an ah six step back
Me seh ah four step fahwahd an ah one step back
Me seh ah one half fahwahd an ah one half back

Me seh di heat ah di night ah come up thru di floor
Black smoke ah rise tho dem nevah did know
Di music ah jam an di young man ah chat
Word fly from him lip like vampire bat

An di gyal dem ah dance an di man dem ah rock
Drink six rum an black an di beat dem ah drop
Darkness descend and di room gone black
Voices ah call seh dem haffi get out

Voices ah call seh dem haffi get out
Screamin begin an di people ah shout
Me seh screamin begin an di people ah shout
Dem ah covah dem head an ah covah dem mouth

Me seh ah two step fahwahd an ah two step back
Me seh ah tree step fahwahd an ah six step back
Me seh ah four step fahwahd an ah one step back
Me seh ah one half fahwahd an ah one half back

Down pun di street yuh see body face down
Pickney fly thru di air an mash up pun di ground
Flames dem ah fly an ah furious red
Bwoy fall from di window an yuh know seh him dead

Gyal fall back inside an we no see her no more
No bright green dress up pon di third floor
Police man come an fireman too
Dem startle dem scared an no know wha fi do

Mudda she ah cry an she nah have no shoes
Man dem ah look but to help dem refuse
Fren dem shock by di scale ah di loss
Black smoke ah billow down there in New Cross

Me seh black smoke ah billow at di house in New Cross
Me seh black smoke ah billow at di house in New Cross
Me seh blood ah goh run for di pain of di loss
Me seh black smoke ah billow at di house in New Cross

Me seh ah left side fahwahd an me right side back
Bust up left side right side haffi change tack
Me seh half de revalushun deh pun de attack
Only half a salushun to de tings dem we lack

Me seh ah two step fahwahd an ah two step back
Me seh ah tree step fahwahd an ah six step back
Me seh ah four step fahwahd an ah one step back
Me seh ah one half fahwahd an ah one half back

# Clearing

He takes my head and places it in a plastic bag

downstairs, two officers stamp their feet
blow into their hands

the windows are cups of water filled with winter

he holds the bag open, searching
for a gaze to meet

cold
thirsts at the bones

he doesn't see me standing there
he doesn't hear me speak

an officer circles the front yard leaning
back to see the smoke

                    or is it steam

is it fire or water that can bring a child back

elide that which is heavy in his hand
and that which watches from the corner of the room

this house is a gas lamp
soot frosts its glasswhite gut

the officer closes his eyes
two blank pennies in a fount

from the bag I watch his face turn away
from the corner his body bending towards mine

+

the officer said – oh, it's very common for culprits to go missing – I said my son isn't a culprit, and how dare he imply it – and one of the officers stood up by the window and looked out – he didn't want to look us full in the eye – he made it clear, he made it clear – from the moment he set foot in the house – the moment he set foot – what he thought of us – and when they come back a few days later – I think the Tuesday, I think the Tuesday – they said what were you wearing on the night of the fire? – I said probably – probably – your new trousers – and he said was you wearing a yellow shirt? – I said yes – Brown shoes? – I said yes – and he took out the items from a plastic bag – he took your things from a plastic bag – and he says does this look like it? Does this look like it belongs to you? – I says yes – and he says do you recognise this key? – I said why don't we try it – and we struggled – and it fit – I'm sorry, I'm so sorry, I'm so sorry – so I said what are you sorry for? I want to see my son – stammer, stammer, they say they don't think it is a good idea – I said, I am your father – I said, I said, I am your father – your father – I want to see you –

              – they led us down to a room  – and on the table there you was – no face, nothing to speak of – I said – I said – this is the body where you found the clothes? – nod, nod – So I said, it must be you – this must be my son

—

You came, dad –

        – I had been lying there all night – and I couldn't move. I
opened my eyes and I was in the house and everything was black, dad
– I had been at the party a few hours and I didn't know anything about
what happened, dad – and I felt someone touch me, but I was stiff, dad
– I never been so stiff before – I tried to say it's me, it's me –  but they
were looking at me so strangely, dad – like he couldn't stand to look at
me – couldn't stand the sight of me – Police always looked at me like
that – and he turned me over – and he took the shirt from under me,
and they wrapped me in a blanket and drove me here – and I was lying
there waiting for you, dad – across the table, there were bodies, dad –
Twisted, dad – no heads –like screaming branches of a tree, dad – loads
of them, loads of them, I swear – and I heard them say – they were
saying –

        And then you came and I was calling out to you, dad
– and I know you heard me because here we are, dad – come back –
don't bury me – I can't stand it – I can barely stand it when the lights
go off – and I'm here – and spend the whole night listening for you dad
– I want to crawl between mum and you – in your bed, in your sheets,
dad– that's the only kind of burying I want –

# Kitchen

I went back to my mother's kitchen:

> peas were soaking on the stove
> and a lettuce was uncurling on
> the counter. A plastic bag
> filled with fish was deflating.
> One of the eyes was pressed
> against the side. seemed to be
> the only thing that heard me.

this kitchen:

> the crack in the window; the spice
> rack with a hundred grubby bottles;
> outside, my brother's underwear
> on the line, a postcard from
> aunty in Antigua, a small shelf
> peopled by Erna Brodber, Gus John.

the door to the bathroom:

> I know that the floor is coldest
> by the door, I know what it's like to come
> in here on a dark morning
> and turn the taps and feel
> the whole house warming up –
> the gradual breath it takes through
> the wallpaper, the carpet, the kettle,
> the dutch pot, the kippers sparking in oil –
> I have crept down through the dark,
> listened to the house open

one red eye and spin it round,
then snort, then fall back to sleep;
I have held this house
in my arms and let it sob
on the bathroom floor, heard it in
the background of a call,
heard it speak a kind of love –

I have watched the street lights shudder
through this bathroom window,
shake themselves to black
and lick the daylight in their fur.
The first ray unencumbered
by the clouds spreads
its rose palm against the window –

I will be that for my brother and mother:

the light touching their faces as she
guts the fish, drains the peas.

# Proof

I came here when I was six –

I was dark-skinned in a thin dress and I loved my grandmother –
she was my mother – and she raised me with my three sisters who
still stand waving me goodbye –

I was the first to come to England, and when I arrived, I knew –
I knew – something had happened to me – I knew that what I saw
in the mirror had been darkened, differently arranged –
when I looked at myself in my new coat and boots I saw – I saw –
something like a net that catches death –

I was the child of two strangers with my last name – who bathed me –
scrubbed me with the seawater at the bottom of their lives –
two ghosts rubbing soap on my shoulders –
two dead people in their house clothes telling me to wash my neck –

I feel – I feel like I have to hold on – and say – and say –
I don't want to die in this country – let me die with my grandmother –
I want to be rotted by the sun –
and I want her shadow to fall along my body –
and I want to be shaded by her grief –
and I want the dogs to hanker for my bones –
I want to be eaten by worms and become an ackee tree –
lord, I said – I said it in such a whisper
I could have put the ground to sleep –

don't let me die in England I said to the pavement –
to the sea-black rain –
and never tell my grandmother why I never called –
never called to say that I thought of her daily –
that I suffered with the weight of what she had freely given –

many nights before this one I wondered what she thought of that –
what she thought of her youngest grandchild who couldn't say that
many nights before this one I tried to forget that I loved her –
turned the pain of her remembrance to the bitter lie that she could not
have loved one such as me and the proof was in the distance –

# Window

When I could no longer see a window to jump from
I remembered the boy, 19, *bound so he could not see the other two.*
When we realised it was only we who remained
he called to us in Creole, "You do not know how to die. See how to die."

As though I had seen the charred yellow soles of his feet myself,
as though I had walked him to the stake myself.

By a great effort he twisted his body in his bonds, sat down,
and placing his feet in the flames, let them burn without uttering a groan.

I remembered him for the rest of my life
which is to say I followed him through the smoke
as though someone had untied his wrists,
taken him on the back of a donkey
to the gully where he was born,

fed him
       *Green bananas?*
                      Green bananas until night fell,

taken him into the house before seeing
that he was half smoke, that he had been floating away,
closed the shutters,
wrapped him in the one good blanket,
kept him separate from the candles,
let him become like the dark blue wall of a house
by the door where the light steps past,
like the mute grease of comers and goers.

*A painting of an old, great king?*

                Old king with a flaking face.

*Spirit on a cave wall?*

                The dye that fixed the yak.


And in the yard, the foreign sea,
armies come turning on a zoetropic mist.


And Mucius Scaevola?


"Greater than Mucius Scaevola…"
sent out of Porsena, so shocking was his bravery.


*His* smooth white body is in the Louvre, turning, saying,
        "How cheap the body is to men."

# NEW CROSS MASSACRE
## 12 DEAD   27 INJURED

PRESS ASSOCIATION

# SUPPORT
# Black Peoples
# Day Of Action

# DEMONSTRATE
## On March 2nd 1981

### Assemble at 10am at
Fordham Park next to Moonshot Community Centre Pagnell Street London SE14

### Demonstration Moves From
439 New Cross Road to Fleet Street, Scotland Yard, House of Commons
and 10 Downing Street ending in Hyde Park

> STAND UP AGAINST THE MASS MURDER OF BLACK PEOPLE
> STAND UP AGAINST ATTACKS BY WHITE RACISTS ON BLACK
> PEOPLE
> STAND UP AGAINST THE BRITISH MOVEMENT, THE NATIONAL
> FRONT AND COLUMN 88
> STAND UP AGAINST THE LIES AND CONFUSION SPREAD BY NEWS-
> PAPERS, RADIO AND TELEVISION
> STAND UP FOR THE RIGHTS OF BLACK PEOPLE TO HAVE THEIR
> PARTIES WITHOUT INTERFERENCE
> WE WILL NOT LET THE POLICE PLAY AROUND WITH OUR LIVES

Issued by the New Cross Massacre Action Committee, c/o 74 Shakespeare Road, London SE24. Tel: 01-737 2268

British Rail and Underground    Nearest Trains: New Cross and New Cross Gate    Buses: 171, 53, 36, 36a, 36b, 141, 177, 21.

**P.T.O.**

# Duppy

I watch them twist back her arm

jerk her head back    flash of the photographer
turns her irises to rings    free flesh    head wet with sweat

The light that evening turned    from blue to siren blue.
Fordham Park packed that afternoon –
chicken sandwich    big coat    money for the bus
cold rain co-steamed    in green and grey
the city parts its lips    speaks the crowd    dodge them boys in blue

Everyone I know

present in the arch of the baton    cracking heads
clamour like battered cod    crackles when bitten
like kids skipping for freedom
cracked puddle    reflects the procession
rude boys moody    like the underside of clouds

No-one will tell me    what happened to my body

I see my picture on a sign    my name
as though the march
were my mother's mantelpiece    Lewisham the frame
every face come in like a cousin
      tall boys carry my empty coffin

*Porky pig, porky pig    ain't you got some graves to dig?*

Heavies in wet leather    calling to regroup
wrestlers turned stewards with umbrellas
icy run-down       fire soup for all

We have transformed this country

into a likkle    dark skin pickney
        bopping for laughs
at carnival    squat him batty
in rich people petunia
drop him patty       pun dem floor

Crowd thick as carnival

once    on my father's shoulders
I wished he would grip
        my rattling heart as tight
as he gripped my calves
I felt the bass through his head
and neck
pound my stomach in its basin
                the sound
chirping    wet    English heat
the louder it is       the closer we are    to home

I follow them late into the night

soak    what little I have left    in soca
drink the last    of the libation    poured at my feet
eat a petal from the bouquet    shaped like my name

The crowd passes through me

Every lord called upon      every church song sung

every psalm and saying
      every aunt chasing duppy

cannot bring us back
nor the speakers
nor the bass    nor the sound

nor the spectre
of the centuries' coming cold
nor Hyde Park Corner    nor the speaker
nor any hosanna
      or channel of peace

# Hiss

Going in when the firefighters left
was like standing on a black beach
with the sea suspended in the walls,
soot suds like a conglomerate of flies.

You kick the weeds and try to piece it back.
Fractured shell? A bone? Bloated antennae?
Flesh thigh spindle, gangrenous pet fish?
An eye or a tiny glaring stone? A seal's tongue?
Or the sour sinew yoking front and hind fin?
Vertebrae or fetters? Bedsheet or slave skin?

The black is coming in from the cold,
rolling up the beach walls, looking for light.

It will enter you if you stand there,
and spend the rest of its time inside you
asking *whatitwas whatitwas whatitwas*
in a vivid hiss heard only by your bones.

# Washing

The silent crowd gathered by the tree wrapped in ribbons. As it neared eleven, they picked up their buckets and cans of paint and walked around the corner to the station. Inside a woman was tearing skin from her fingers with her teeth. She stared. Someone gave her a yellow cloth and gestured that she stand.

*"In Birmingham, there had been a West Indian Christmas party that lasted nine days."*

The silent crowd had brought coca-cola, vinegar, a three-pack of firm toothbrushes, a Henry Hoover.

*"I went down to the cafe and played space invaders."*

Beginning in the far corner: three-year-old with a feather duster and her sister with a can of Pledge and their aunty stepping onto the bolted-down bench in her flip-flops to reach the windows and the tall one coiling all the cobwebs with their hands and another changing the flickering bulbs and another pouring water into the cheese plants.

*"I think I could have brought plastic cups down in a stack."*

More came, with sage and agarwood and tarot cards and made a tiny altar by the chairs where the bleeding, the roofless, the broken-hearted and the vengeful sat, watching them scrub the floor and the skirting boards, using their gloved nails to pick at the dried muck.

*"When the policeman went everything was peaceful, for it was pure youths down there."*

Then the silent crowd opened a tin of paint. They were going to make this very beautiful. When everything was white - even the windows, even the cracked biros provided - they carried in pews and fresh flowers and helped each other change their clothes.

*"They asked me about the sound, about the ownership of the sound."*

And when the canon came with his swinging smoke he strode past the crowd to the window where the officer sat, touched the painted glass with his holy fingers, shut his eyes and murmured a blessing. We assume the officer bowed his head.

## Stone

autumn
in all its orange dresses    sipping rain in Fordham Park

A tyre swing
eclipses the world    within    its hoop

I have found the stone    with the names of all the dead

I sit

and meet the stone's    cold    pink mirror

                              garbled sun
thirteen names

                    every year

I hear summer    ask    how autumn
can endure
winter's undoing

# Apple

And so, the revolutionary had a birthday party.
Everyone gathered around the cake,
a single pink candle for all those years.
Don't you love how they decided mid-meal
to lean into each other, peer into the photo,
don't you love that there is chicken grease
from the early part of this century,
that it was cooked at the revolutionary's house
on Albert Road, that someone living
might recall the smell of the lentils,
the pop of the grilled tomatoes,

the particular apple
they ate in slices having sat back,
wiped the cake knife on the edge
of the plate, peeled its long green skin,
and cut the pieces into pages,
left it ageing on the plate –
John, Sarah, Linton, Sharmilla, Gus,
Abdul, Lawrence, Wole, Akua, Carol,
Jo, Susan, Barbara –

don't you love those pieces of apple,
the brown photograph they have become,
don't you love that there is nothing
remarkable here, nothing that would
startle a state, but that it has been kept
anyway, noted, dated, numbered, placed
in acid-free Japanese boxes and lovingly
(as is tradition) laid without a casket.

# Songbook II

How many times has Miss D died?
How many times has she given us life
How many children does miss D have?
As many as the people hearing this song

    Hearing this song
    I said they're hearing this song
    I said they're listening in from beyond

    Hearing this song
    I said they're hearing this song
    They're listening in from beyond

How many lovers has Miss D had?
As many as there are leaves on the trees
How many places has Miss D lived?
As many as there are names on the map

    Names on the map
    As there are names on the map
    As there are places that you can belong

    Names on the map
    As there are names on the map
    As there are places that you can belong

How many times has Miss D died?
As often as there have been babies born
How many times will she die once more?
As long as things are worth dying for

And she came up in the morning
And she went down in the evening
And she came up with the rising of the sun

And she came up in the morning
And she went down in the evening
And when I turn around she was gone

How many times have you seen her since?
Never again, not in the same way
She used to be down in Deptford market
Laughing with the sellers all day

Haggling fish, I said she's haggling rice
I said she's good at driving down price

Haggling fish, I said she's haggling rice
I said she's good at driving down price

I haven't seen her, nor have you
Not since the fire at 439
I heard her daughter was gone for days
They wouldn't let her see the remains

And she came up in the morning
And she went down in the evening
And she came up with the rising of the sun

And she came up in the morning
And she went down in the evening
And when I turn around she was gone

And when I turn around she was gone
And when I turn around she was gone
And when I turn around she was gone

*"Also, I think the thing about the current moment and loss is the sense that we don't yet have the thing, but we already fear losing it."*\*

---

\*Text message from Sita, 9 June 2017, 22.02PM

# Pem-People

We have come to light a candle for you
Naomi, at the pop-up shop in Peckham.

We lay out red and green cloth, fairy lights,
bring a steaming pot of beans to share.

A woman stands in the centre.
Your death, she says, proves

that there is no difference between the one
you love and the one who kills you.

A man in a grey suit speaks from his seat,
saying he knew you. He is angry, talking of how you

loved tennis, the Williams Sisters
with their braids and their power, white-skirted

black thunder life-giving on the green.
He says you were as fierce as that.

Do we clap? Okay, we do. Then he asks for one
minute's silence above the evening traffic,

dancehall, the people in the room above us,
and it is silent here – the minute comes and

passes and still it is silent. I take a yellow
Post-it note and try to write something true

but really I am hungry and tired, really
I have nothing, really I want to eat the bean stew alone

and watch Venus throw her serve across YouTube
until it takes me somewhere I did not intend.

# Pace

I have seen the light you've seen
and my body has been where yours has been
some part of me resides where you reside
we've swapped presences and parting –

I have seen what you have seen
become the part of you I stood beside
passing friend with green eyes
I now reside where you reside –

hello, you standing there to the left of me
you in the heart of those hearing me read
further ahead on the road we are walking
there in the shadow performing in front of me –

you in the rhythm that's always unfolding
you are a question that's always been asked
who are we now and what are we wanting
from the voices you heard, the presences there –

how do we ask the quiet you've left
what voice you recalled
whose hand you were holding?

# Tympanum

Wood smoke of black Anglicans behind the body.
As he was in life, he is heavy. Pallbearers lock knees
against the weight and tilt the coffin over the lip.
The tips of my father's fingers guide me by the back of the head.
Blown cheek of the roof, ulcer and teal, gas pipe and cherub.
The radiator prays for warmth. As in life, my uncle's body
is raised like a newborn. People are gentle with him, speak slowly.
Black feathered congregation missed breakfast sharpening their shoes.
My cousin throws a low grin between the pews and we play
muffled *had*, skidding along the rows as though sitting still.
Until the singing, I had been thinking of that warm night
legs slung over either side of the church wall, ankles locked
with my lover drinking Stella, the song said I am here,
I don't have to worry, you can see your tears. Can I open my mouth
and say such things, can I let this song see me cry?
My cousin went up to the body, alone, and looked.
She turned to me. The answer, as it is in heaven:
something about a child with its hands over its face.

# Ha-my-ca

My mother and her boyfriend had gone
to see a man about a dog again.
The taxi driver turned to me and asked
whether I knew that 'Jamaica' was from Spanish,
*ha-my-ca*, he said, *ha-my-ca*.
Had I asked what name it had before
I might have learned a word for my body, not felt so alone
later, dropping into that cold green pool at the hotel;
low season, no-one but us on the deckchairs all day
until sunfall when I let my swimsuit slip down my shoulder,
float on my back, starbathe under ursa minor.
This hour,
when Ocho Rios smiles between the trees like a gold-tooth aunty,
I let my swimsuit slip to my waist, let the evening tongs
twist my nipples, make them cold and constellate.
In these late hours I have learned to spit pool water
like a cartoon fish, how to flounder at the bottom
of the pool like a tabloid news story, how to make my glass
of coke last all day so that only now am I groping for it
in the dark, sucking its last flat buzz. The pool lights come on.
I clamber onto the lilo with its pink panther head,
let my swimsuit slip down my legs, bubble up behind me,
faff and squeak below the sole light in the hotel:
five stories up, my mother appears on the balcony,
hanging something wet to dry / I leap into the water,
bob naked, like a brown bottle with a sodden note.
I learned of self and other when my waist left the water
and my mother, up there in the dark, waited another hour
before she called us up. She and he barely touched us
when we came, wet, with wrinkled hands and feet.

*Ha-my-ca.* Package deal; three nights in *Ochi* –
One, the kid undresses in the darkening *ha.*
Two, in its hands, soft water, it parts on *my.*
Three, to re-surface, to twin at the tail on *ca.*
That other way of saying it, that other way to understand.

*"...the mutability of a body defined as inexhaustibly interchangeable, an inhabitation of the virtually uninhabitable, being within the zone of non-being.*"*

---

*C. Riley Snorton, *Black on Both Sides*

# Kombucha

I have learned to drink of this like a fine kombucha. This body-warm drink, mud at the bottom of the mooncup. For a year I carried you with me. The sign at the storage unit said 'no food, no perishables', but I kept you in that box, each bottle in the little clay tray. The blood was growing one grey bubble into the neck of the bottle. It was you. As you as you are. Blood fur from the time your body was made. They say that we exist inside our mother's sac of eggs when she is but a sac of eggs laid inside her mother. When I stare at these bottles, it's blood that has been three times enlarged. Who says we have no genealogy? Who says that if I line them up, as ornaments, a blood archive, then it isn't like us having had a child? The last I have of you: old blood, homebrew.

# Peg

Tonight we are boys together. Now I understand
why for brothers postcodes rule. These looks
are not friendly. Two boys, one suspiciously short,
touching elbows as we walk past the KFC,
down Coldharbour Lane, with streets lit
like an outdoor stage; under the bridge, past the
behemoth of Somerleyton, past the
houses that have been empty since the eighties;
I turn to look at death painted fifty feet high,
a skeletal foot on each building, birds following
a fatalistic hand. We walk by the off license,
past Valencia, deserted, down to the dark origin
of Shakespeare Road.

This bus stop might be the first outpost to the underworld.
It's a summer night and you smell good.
Of yourself. Nut-like. Sour dough sweat.
We go to the top deck and sit up front.
The bus heaves past Loughborough, to Camberwell,
to the green, buzzing with students drunk on Friday,
drunk on art and trendy and young; wine bottle young,
rollie-young, tight, flat-chested young. I follow you down,
I follow you up to the stairs to your flat, your back,
your hips, up, to a bedroom overlooking South London,
                              it whispers, undress,
                    undress, we don't need to speak –
speak with your clothes, say it in the sound of your shirt
falling to the floor; we agreed on this hours ago.
We had the idea years ago. Now we are boys together. Bend.

# Pride

I am seventeen, summer is still gold clap of hot body
and hot body. Blue sky fries the tiny sun.
I kiss myself for courage and duck into the parade.
Two dykes smiling like young mothers ask me my name.
Our gazes lock on love, our slow wend among the cut offs,
wrecked docs, glinting nose rings, heads shaved to skin,
a stranger's hand on my shoulder became a loving mouth
pressing its heat into mine, urgent tongue searching for a place
to pass the root in that way, to go knuckle deep in another,
in a third way sucking white sap directly
and watering the teat, going out unshowered but for that fresh sweat –

am I the steaming black street, am I the banner and the band, the crush,
lilting ale, tipsy hug, charged flesh and open eye

That was then          heading to First Out when it was us on the menu,
salad of fierce look and full power lasagne, speaking with full mouth:
queer, lesbian, dyke. Offender of no gender. Failed woman.
Swamp. Black flag. Bleach blonde. Sunday Happy Sunday.
What it was to me then, those bare arms, to have found them at last,
below a slow float, that heat, that mood, that pride.

My body taps me on the heart when someone in soft leather swims
into my ken, that smell of squat and underground and every other lover,
scent that throws off shame – these days I pass you in the street,
though I want to turn around and thank you for the tongue in my throat,
for this thick and practiced ass and cunt, for my plaited scars and flat nipples.

They call this a city, I call it the dark between two bodies.

JAMES O'BRIEN: *Do you understand why the authorities have not been able to confirm that definitively to you?*

NAZANIN AKLANI: *Yes, because they let them burn for too long. You know, James, what's more horrendous than getting burned alive? You know, you ask yourself is there anything worse? And I'm afraid there is, you know. Having no remains.\**

*BBC Newsnight, July 12 2017

# Sentence

If mum is in the living room / sister in the bathroom / then sentence
says / morning / the two have not yet / said their first words –

If mum is in the bedroom / sister in the bedroom /
then it is evening / and sentence says / sister is leaning against the
door, cross-legged / drawing –

If the two are in the kitchen / best friend also /
unzipping fish spine from / its studded silver flesh / then sentence says –

the wound around the waist of the house punctured / full of indoor
exits that do not close behind you / stairs / take you back to the start
/ what you were running from / dark warps the frame –

the people have taken their hands away from their eyes / and have
stapled their mothers and sisters to the underpass wall / their cousins
and brothers and lovers to the underpass wall / only the missing –
never the dead – to the underpass wall.

Not rivers, towers of blood.

# Ark II

Night meets me near Ladbroke Grove / with a warm June morning in my hands / in the story I am trying to tell / what doesn't fit is part of the hole / a heart split across its middle reveals a pool / a painted minaret shelters St. Anthony / I am here alone without the silent march / I will act natural in this freezing underpass / sketchier than I remember / exercise a little memorial discipline / not jump / or be seen to write this down / "The Innocence of Children", by Molly aged 18 months / "Pets we'er killed too" / "Every morning rise with the people" / "Glass trees have no roots" / the vents make it smell like someone's kitchen / I wish I had brought a dishful of candles / a lighter at least / seriously / our lady of perpetual help / tinsel / strawberry drink

\*

Night meets me at the end of the road / with a warm June morning in my hands / in the story I am trying to tell / Michael Smithyman murdered his girlfriend in the 90s / claimed to witness the fire in New Cross / transitioned in prison to Michelle / denied the claim / ■■■■■■■ / has no recollection / no further meaningful lines of enquiry / the story lives inside the house / in a video the anchor pulls the curtains closed in a reconstructed morning / a friend sends me a link to the burning tower effigy / in the 80s people sent letters / I am not convinced the people in the video actually find themselves funny / I read about Smithyman again / I wish it wasn't so soon / I wish the outcome mattered / I wish I had watched the whole inquiry / I wish I could relax / around the man claiming to be the official underpass muralist / asking me why I have no money / the columns read: ♥♥♥♥♥♥♥ / S T R E N G T H

# Chemical

And all of their ghosts are burning
above the city. Some fires burn
pink as damaged blossom.
Those broken vessels, bruised, lit
and upward streaking, rose-hot capillaries
ignite the dead's ragged cloth and unshrooms
them to gas. Screaming crackle. Frayed spirit,
unbecoming black we think makes up the unseen,
but that black is the last twisted shape
their bodies will take. The floor, the rooms,
liquid windows part absence, part gas.
And then the wind breathes sideways:
their soot is scattered, ghosts of the now-gone
dragged out of hereafter back to tonight,
back to the cold air making its way towards
a darker past, the true past, there at spirit level.

# Blank

_____ was loved by all, loved more now that –

    *Thousands of people are calling on the government to allow him to stay.*

It wasn't _____'s fault, different papers gave different figures –

    *He raced towards the ferocious blaze which engulfed his*
    *neighbour's home.*

_____ had been lying face-down when the fire-fighters –

    *After hearing screams of terror from those trapped inside.*

No-one recognised the body, no-one had anything to say to –

    *He, who has lived in the UK for 16 years,*
    *is facing deportation and fears for his safety.*

_____ ran back in when suddenly –
_____ was seen from the inside, waiting at the window –

    *He ran to the house in his bare feet.*

It said that several thousand people marched in the rain from –
And now what is there, _____? What do we have to show for –

    *He called up to the youngsters to jump and he would catch them.*

We don't know anything about that. Nobody said anything about –
It said that you were loved _____, and you were always gonna –

*Grandmother, 47, and grandfather, 56, died at the scene.*

The family of _____ today issued this statement –
The family of _____ ask for your respect –

*Organisers hope to deliver the petition to the Home Secretary.*

It-has-nothing-to-do-with-us today issued this statement:
those involved have defended their actions and been given /
been given / acquitted / retired with full pay / charged / acquitted /
desk duty / retired with full pay / been given / been given –

*Let's save this gentle giant.*

I read that you were loved, I read that you were –
I read about you_____, I read that you were –

# Baccy

I stop work and go downstairs
for the house meeting. Make tea.
Shake Hobnobs onto a plate,
mind like a cigarette, tethered to '81.

We need to discuss whether we
open the door to our neighbour
when he asks for milk and tobacco.

Our fridge is full of tupperware,
mince with its mossy grey hair
standing up on end. Beignet mix
with green and white acne.
Ham hock and beetroot overcome
by clouds. Clotted cream like a cracked
heel in the desert.

He asks for the earth.

If he comes again,
we are to give him     this much,
our fingers pinch the air,
                              and this much,
we part our hands about the height of a heart.

# Losers

We losers are winning now that the losers have lost.
The moaning is getting annoying, let's get back to the winning.
The thing that we won when the losers were kneeling and begging,
before they came with their losing and coming to us with the cost.

The looser it is the riper it is for the losing. My sorrow lets loose
on the nation, opens its arms to the weeping, a basket of beans
for the wounded, nappies and sugar and fish cakes and coupons
are paving the road for the moving: we winners with winners
And losers out there with their losing.

To lose and to lose. To be last in the lotto of loss. I send my sorrow
to mingle with yours. To meet at the pub and lessen the pain of your losing.
It's the only question we ask. Will anyone lessen the losing?
Will anyone lessen the loss?

You can't make the boss listen to us, the boss never spends
lunchtime with us, only when profit and cost and money or
money or us comes into the balance and toss of a coin is enough.
I have school but I don't have a house. My mother's confused

as to how I can shout the answers to Mastermind but nothing
is working out. "The English have won in the lotto of life" –
aren't we all English now? This coast is great 'cos our cots were in it,
our passport as good as it got. Now someone else wins the lot.

You're either or neither or not. There's no middle ground,
there's no way round and some of us gave all we got.
Get lost with your truth and your news which never speaks for our lot.
We lessen the loss with a curry, a pint and a curry for mummy,

who can't understand all the fuss, she can't understand why we must.

Back in her day it wouldn't have stood, back when the great and the good could chill a nation to frost, could ration and batter and murder the young and never be seen to have lost.

I try to ensure I can always recall the particular moment we lost, it slips through my fingers at most. Another, another, the memory conjured and lost. Losing and losing and loss. Never recouping the cost.

# Flowers

Will anybody speak of this
the way the flowers do,
the way the common speaks
of the fearless dying leaves?

Will anybody speak of this
the way the common does,
the way the fearless dying leaves
speak of the coming cold?

Will anybody speak of this
the way the fearless dying leaves
speak of the coming cold
and the quiet it will bring?

Will anybody speak of this
the coming of the cold,
the quiet it will bring,
the fire we beheld?

Will anybody speak of this
the quiet it will bring
the fire we beheld,
the garlands at the gate?

Will anybody speak of this
the fire we beheld
the garlands at the gate,
the way the flowers do?

# Notes

'Songbook' is after Linton Kwesi Johnson's 'New Crass Massakah', 1981.

Image of poster detailing the Black People's Day of Action was created by the New Cross Massacre Action Committee, 1981.

In 'Window' the italicised text is from C.L.R. James's *Black Jacobins*, p.361 (from Lemonnier-Delafosse, *Second Campagne de Saint-Domingue précédée de souvenirs historiques et succints de la premiére campagne*, Paris, 1846).

'Hiss' borrows from Aimé Césaire's *Notebook of a Return to My Native Land* (Bloodaxe, 1995).

'Washing' borrows lines from the fact-finding commission conducted by the New Cross Massacre Action Committee. Some have been altered to maintain confidentiality.

Names referenced in 'Apple' are from several photos held at the George Padmore Institute showing celebrations of John La Rose's birthday as well as other gatherings.

The image of the sign outside 439 New Cross Road is taken from a short contemporary film whose provenance has not been established.

The image depicting the vigil in 1982 was taken by Julian Stapleton and shows family members of the New Cross Fire victims.

'Pem-People' is after the community space in Peckham where a memorial was held for Naomi Hersi, a black trans-woman who was found murdered in 2018.

'Pace' was the pen name of Thomas Crosby, a young poet who passed in 2016. His name and memory is spray painted on a shopfront in East London.

'Sentence' is after Khadija Saye, a victim of the Grenfell fire.

'Ark II' references a BBC article from 3 November 2015 entitled 'Met Police "halted probe" into killer Michael Smithyman's confessions', as well as the Grenfell Tower burning effigy, a video of which emerged in 2018.

'Blank' borrows lines from an article in the *Manchester Weekly News*, 'Please Let Blaze Hero Stay in UK Petition', March 16 2017.

# Acknowledgements

An early version of *Surge* first appeared in *Beacon of Hope* (New Beacon, 2016). An essay containing 'Songbook' was published by *Poetry Review*. 'Peg' first appeared in *English Breakfast* (Math Paper Press, 2013). 'Proof' originally appeared in *Wasafiri Magazine*. These poems were first read at the Last Word Festival at the Roundhouse in Camden, the Hay Festival in Segovia, Spain, and Contains Strong Language in Hull.

This book is based on the archives collected by family members, friends and activists who survived the New Cross Fire. I'd like to acknowledge the thirteen dead as well as the fourteenth who took his life later on: Patricia Johnson, Yvonne Ruddock, Paul Ruddock, Glen Powell, Gerry Francis, Owen Thompson, Andrew Gooding, Lloyd Hall, Anthony Berbeck, Lillian Henry, Peter Campbell, Humphrey Brown, Patrick Cummings, Steve Collins. I have listened to the words and worked from the actions of Sybil Phoenix, Darcus Howe, John La Rose, Vron Ware, and countless people who informally discussed their memories of that period with me after readings.

I would also like to acknowledge the numerous groups who worked to create the memorials and events I draw on in this book. The walks and demonstrations I attended, in particular the silent march for Grenfell, were made possible by the activism and dedication of others, including the Grenfell Action Group and Justice 4 Grenfell.

Thanks to:

Speaking Volumes – Sharmilla Beezmohun, Nick Chapman and Sarah Sanders – for all the work they have put in to helping me develop and for commissioning the residency that sparked this book; the George Padmore Institute and New Beacon Books – Sarah Garrod and Sarah White – for all their support and assistance in the archive and in the book shop; LAGNA archive in Bishopsgate; The Carmelites – the delightful bunch who attended my queer archives and poetry course, and in doing so helped me understand what this collection was about. Massive thanks to Mayday Rooms and Statewatch. Many thanks to long-time friends Kayo Chingonyi, Yemisi Blake and Inua Ellams. Thanks Parisa Ebrahimi for all of the early encouragement and interest. Thanks also to Yaddo for time and space, to the K Blundell Trust and the judges of the Ted Hughes Award 2017. Much appreciation to The Complete Works, as ever, and to Kate Birch at IS&T for her continued enthusiasm and support. Many thanks to the crew who worked on the film that accompanied the early scratch show *Surge: Side A*: Harley Yeung Kurylowski, Tabitha Benjamin and Rufai Ajala, and to everyone at Philomela's Chorus. Thanks to Rex Obano and Selina Thompson for their invaluable advice. Finally, thanks to my friends: Sita Balani, Melissa Cespedes del Sur, Deborah Grayson, Nazmia Jamal and Natasha Nkonde, for their support over the years.